Young Learner's

Number

Writing Book

1-20

1

Giraffe

2

Caps

3

Cushions

4

Balls

Trace and Learn: |

Date: ____________ Grade: ____________ Teacher's Signature: ______________

Practice Time!

Colour the lotus with pink and green colours.

Date: ____________ Grade: ____________ Teacher's Signature: ______________

Trace and Learn: 2

Date: __________ Grade: __________ Teacher's Signature: __________

Practice Time!

Colour number '1' in red colour and number '2' in blue colour.

Date: ___________ Grade: ___________ Teacher's Signature: ___________

Trace and Learn: 3

Date: ___________ Grade: __________ Teacher's Signature: ____________

Practice Time!

Write the number of objects.

Date: ____________ Grade: ____________ Teacher's Signature: ______________

Trace and Learn: 4

4	4	4	4	4	4	4	4	4
4	4	4	4	4	4	4	4	4
4	4	4	4	4	4	4	4	4
4	4	4	4	4	4	4	4	4
4	4	4	4	4	4	4	4	4
4	4	4	4	4	4	4	4	4
4	4	4	4	4	4	4	4	4

Date: ____________ Grade: ___________ Teacher's Signature: _____________

Practice Time!

Count the books and circle the correct number.

2 3 4

Date: ____________ Grade: ___________ Teacher's Signature: _____________

Trace and Learn: 5

5	5	5	5	5	5	5	5	5
5	5	5	5	5	5	5	5	5
5	5	5	5	5	5	5	5	5
5	5	5	5	5	5	5	5	5
5	5	5	5	5	5	5	5	5
5	5	5	5	5	5	5	5	5
5	5	5	5	5	5	5	5	5

Date: ____________ Grade: ___________ Teacher's Signature: ____________

Practice Time!

Match each apple to its correct tree.

2 5 2 5 1 4 3 3 1 4

Date: ___________ Grade: ___________ Teacher's Signature: ___________

Date: ___________ Grade: __________ Teacher's Signature: ____________

Practice Time!

Count and write the number of swing seats in each carousel.

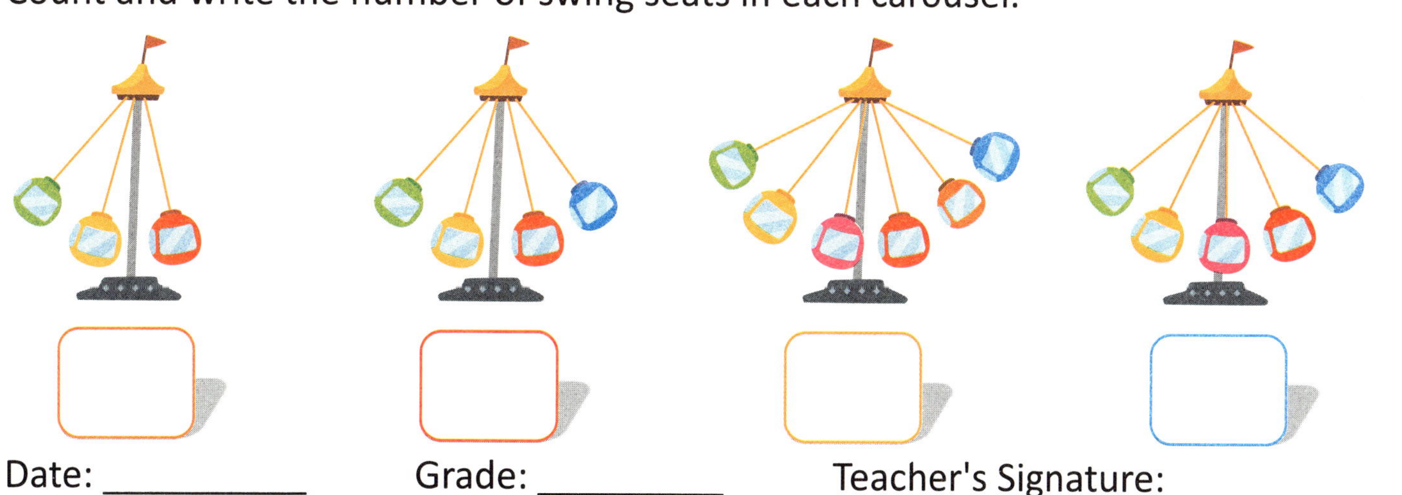

Date: ___________ Grade: ___________ Teacher's Signature: _____________

Date: ____________ Grade: ___________ Teacher's Signature: _____________

Practice Time!

How many are there?

4
7
6
5

6
7
3
5

5
6
4
7

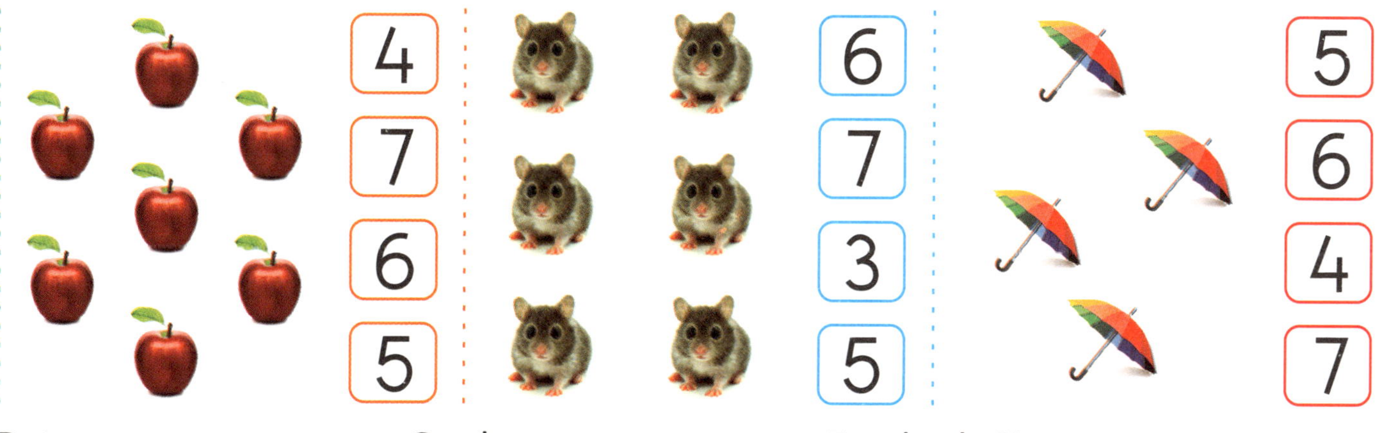

Date: ____________ Grade: ____________ Teacher's Signature: ______________

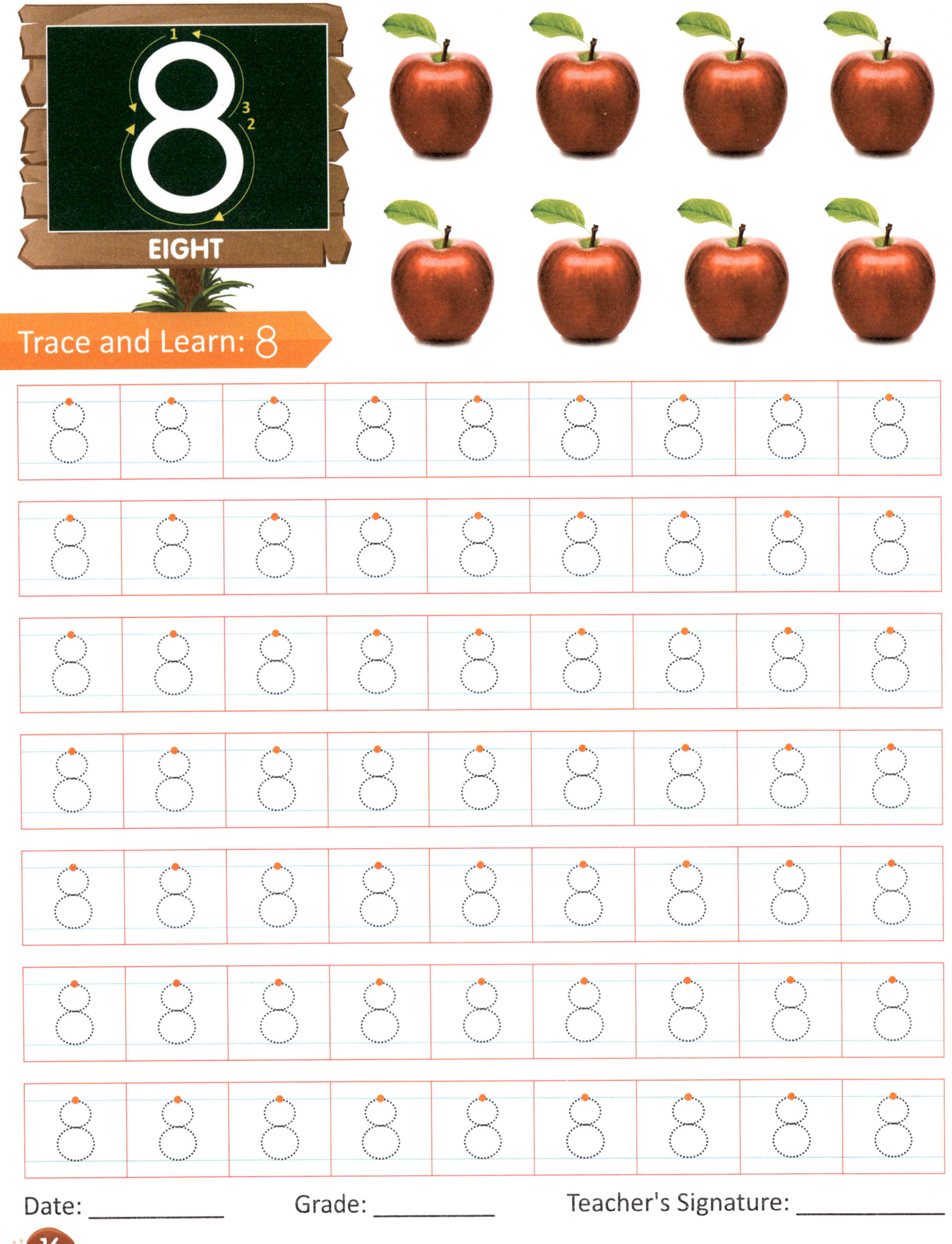

Date: ___________ Grade: ___________ Teacher's Signature: ___________

Practice Time!

Complete the series.

Date: ___________ Grade: ___________ Teacher's Signature: ___________

Date: ____________ Grade: ___________ Teacher's Signature: _____________

Practice Time!

Count the cakes and write the answer in the given box.

Date: ___________ Grade: ___________ Teacher's Signature: ___________

Date: ___________ Grade: ___________ Teacher's Signature: ___________

Practice Time!

Help 'I' reach '0' to make 'I0'.

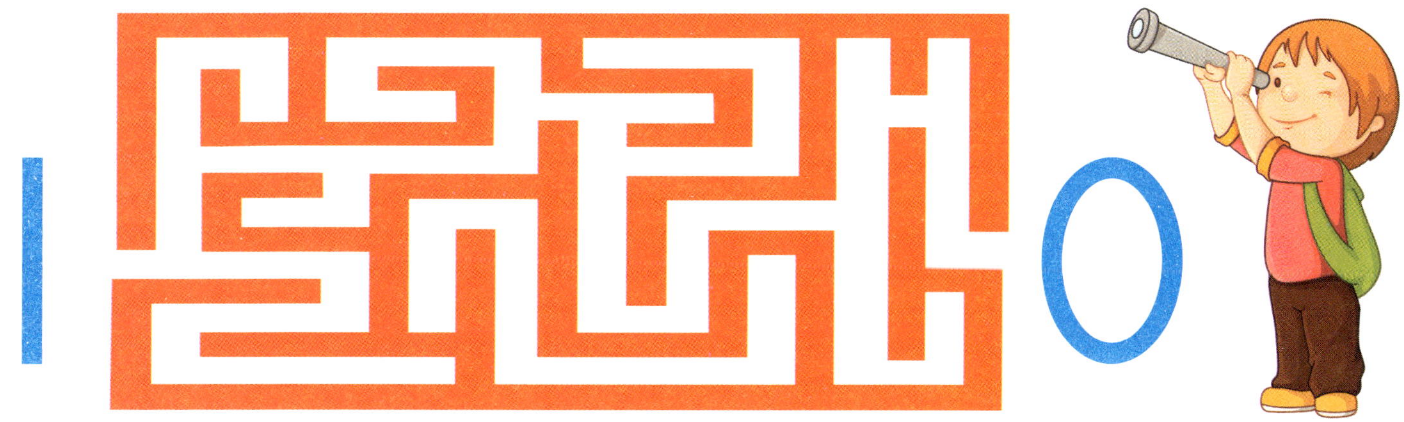

Date: ___________ Grade: ___________ Teacher's Signature: ______________

Date: ___________ Grade: __________ Teacher's Signature: ____________

Date: ____________ Grade: ___________ Teacher's Signature: _____________

13

THIRTEEN

Practice Time: 13

13	13	13	13	13	13	13	13	13
13								
13								
13								
13								
13								
13								

Date: ____________ Grade: ____________ Teacher's Signature: ____________

Date: ____________ Grade: ____________ Teacher's Signature: ______________

Date: ____________ Grade: __________ Teacher's Signature: ______________

Practice Time: 16

16	16	16	16	16	16	16	16	16
16								
16								
16								
16								
16								
16								

Date: ___________ Grade: ___________ Teacher's Signature: ___________

Date: ____________ Grade: ____________ Teacher's Signature: ____________

Date: ____________ Grade: ____________ Teacher's Signature: ______________

Practice Time: 19

19	19	19	19	19	19	19	19	19
19								
19								
19								
19								
19								
19								

Date: ____________ Grade: ____________ Teacher's Signature: ____________

Practice Time: 20

20	20	20	20	20	20	20	20	20
20								
20								
20								
20								
20								
20								

Date: ____________ Grade: ___________ Teacher's Signature: _____________

Activity Time

How many birds are flying?

How many birds are eating food?

How many birds are sitting?